EVERY MORNING WHEN I RISE, HELP ME TO KEEP MY MIND ON JESUS

EVERY MORNING WHEN I RISE, HELP ME TO KEEP MY MIND ON JESUS

Deborah Riley

Copyright © 2020 by Deborah Riley.

Library of Congress Control Number:		2020904470
ISBN:	Hardcover	978-1-7960-9245-5
	Softcover	978-1-7960-9244-8
	eBook	978-1-7960-9243-1

All rights reserved. No part of this book may be reproduced or transmitted in any form or by any means, electronic or mechanical, including photocopying, recording, or by any information storage and retrieval system, without permission in writing from the copyright owner.

Any people depicted in stock imagery provided by Getty Images are models, and such images are being used for illustrative purposes only.
Certain stock imagery © Getty Images.

Print information available on the last page.

Rev. date: 03/05/2020

To order additional copies of this book, contact:
Xlibris
1-888-795-4274
www.Xlibris.com
Orders@Xlibris.com
809603

Scripture taken from the New King James Version®. Copyright © 1982 by Thomas Nelson. Used by permission. All rights reserved.

Scripture quotations are taken from the Holy Bible, New Living Translation, copyright © 1996, 2004, 2015 by Tyndale House Foundation. Used by permission of Tyndale House Publishers, Inc., Carol Stream, Illinois 60188. All rights reserved.

Scripture quotations marked AMP are from The Amplified Bible, Old Testament copyright © 1965, 1987 by the Zondervan Corporation. The Amplified Bible, New Testament copyright © 1954, 1958, 1987 by The Lockman Foundation. Used by permission. All rights reserved.

Scripture quotations marked KJV are from the Holy Bible, King James Version (Authorized Version). First published in 1611. Quoted from the KJV Classic Reference Bible, Copyright © 1983 by The Zondervan Corporation.

Scripture taken from the Holy Bible, NEW INTERNATIONAL READER'S VERSION®.Copyright © 1996, 1998 Biblica. All rights reserved throughout the world. Used by permission of Biblica.

THE HOLY BIBLE, NEW INTERNATIONAL VERSION®, NIV® Copyright © 1973, 1978, 1984, 2011 by Biblica, Inc.® Used by permission. All rights reserved worldwide.

Scripture quotations from the Revised Standard Version of the Bible, copyright © 1946, 1952, and 1971 the Division of Christian Education of the National Council of the Churches of Christ in the United States of America. Used by permission. All rights reserved.

The Holy Bible, English Standard Version (ESV) is adapted from the Revised Standard Version of the Bible, copyright Division of Christian Education of the National Council of the Churches of Christ in the U.S.A. All rights reserved.

Scripture taken from The Voice™. Copyright © 2008 by Ecclesia Bible Society. Used by permission. All rights reserved.

Scripture quotations marked TPT are from The Passion Translation®. Copyright © 2017, 2018 by Passion & Fire Ministries, Inc. Used by permission. All rights reserved. ThePassionTranslation.com.

EVERY MORNING WHEN I RISE, HELP ME TO KEEP MY MIND ON JESUS

The Lord spoke to me and said to "begin to write prayers based upon scriptures from *My Word for women*." So the following is in response to God's direction for this devotional book. Thus, it is my prayer that the passages of scripture from His Word and the prayers of faith and faith declarations that follow are heartfelt and nurturing to the mind, body, soul, and spirit of its readers.

I begin this devotional with the following prayer:

A Daily Morning Prayer

Father, God, in the mighty name of Jesus, I thank You for this day. I acknowledge that this is the day that you have made, and I will rejoice today and be glad in it. Father, God, as I begin this time of prayer, I ask that You would forgive me for anything I have said or thought that was not pleasing to You. I thank You for waking me to a new day, never seen before, that affords me new mercies and grace that can only come from You. Loving Father, I am so blessed because You are a forgiving and an understanding God. You have done so much for me, and You continue to bless me daily even the more.

Father, God, keep me safe today and always from all danger and harm. Father, God, I ask for Your help in starting me off in this day with a new attitude and lots of gratitude for all You have done for me. May I make the very best of each and every day that You give me. Help me to keep my mind clear so that I can hear from You. The Word of God says in Isaiah 26, "You will keep him in perfect peace, whose mind is stayed on You, because he trusts in You." I "trust in the Lord Jehovah."

Heavenly Father, help me to not complain and be in despair over things I have no control over. Your Word says I am not to be anxious for nothing, but in every situation and circumstance by prayer make my requests known to You. Father God, continue to use me to do Your will and for Your glory. Continue to bless me so that I may be a blessing to others. Strengthen me and keep me strong. Keep me lifted up so that I may be an encouragement to others. I love You, Jesus ! Amen!

CONTENTS

Day 1	The Power of God's Wisdom	1
Day 2	#iGrace	3
Day 3	It Is All for His Glory	5
Day 4	God with Us	7
Day 5	Walk Wisely	9
Day 6	Just Keep on Praying	11
Day 7	Worship the Holy God	13
Day 8	Know God's Plan for Your Life	15
Day 9	Be an Obedient Servant	17
Day 10	There Was No King Like Josiah	19
Day 11	"Just Git Err Done"	21
Day 12	Do Not Get So Big and Forget God	23
Day 13	There Is God, Who Knows All About Me	25
Day 14	Full Joy and Pleasures of God Forevermore	27
Day 15	Wisdom	29
Day 16	God, Give Us Wisdom for Prosperity	31
Day 17	Nehemiah's Prayer for a Nation	33
Day 18	By My Spirit	36
Day 19	We Fight in the Power of His Might	38
Day 20	Prayer of Faith and Strength for the Church	40
Day 21	His Peace Keeps Me	42
Day 22	So, Whose Report Do You Believe?	44

Day 23	Why We Can Believe the Report of the Lord	47
Day 24	I Give You Jesus	50
Day 25	God Wants the Best for Us	52
Day 26	God Wants to Increase You More	54
Day 27	To Know Him	56
Day 28	Do You Know What God Has Planned for You?	58
Day 29	I Will Follow God's Plan	60
Day 30	Great God, Great God, Great God!	62
Day 31	Glory, Honor, and Praise to Our God	64
Day 32	About the Author	67

DAY 1

The Power of God's Wisdom

Proverbs 3:19– 22 (NKJV)

Allow God's Word from the book of Proverbs to minister to you. The Word says,

The LORD by wisdom founded the earth; By understanding He established the heavens; By His knowledge the depths were broken up, And clouds drop down the dew. My son, let them not depart from your eyes—Keep sound wisdom and discretion; So they will be life to your soul And grace to your neck.

"He Is Wisdom"

Here I believe that the Lord is speaking to our hearts about how important His wisdom and understanding is to us. His wisdom is life sustaining and provides protection. How meticulous is our God, so much so that by His wisdom He created the world and us in it? Why would we not want His wisdom to guide us through the cares of this life each moment throughout our day?

The same wisdom that founded the earth and established the heavens comes from the same God that gives us His knowledge, His wisdom, and His understanding.

Who would not want His wisdom and understanding? God has given us what we need to live a good life. A life free from worry and despair over the cares of life. God has given us His wisdom, understanding, and knowledge, all just for the asking. This is a great benefit to those who have accepted Christ as their Lord and Savior. It is indeed an added benefit to those who are in the right relationship with God, having received salvation. In this Proverb, Solomon instructs His son to not allow God's wisdom, knowledge, and understanding to depart from him. So, dear daughters of God, do not allow wisdom to depart from you.

Prayer of Faith

Lord, you have freely made available to all who believe in You the benefit of Your wisdom. Thank you, Father, for this great benefit. Father, may I never be without Your wisdom leading and guiding me through the crucible of life. The Word of God says that "many are the afflictions of the righteous" and that You deliver us from them all (Ps. 34:19).

It is only because of Your wisdom that I am able to navigate through these afflictions. Help me to know Your voice, receive Your instruction, and to know that You only want what is best for me. Help me to trust You completely as Your Word says in Proverbs 3:5.

Holy Spirit, help me to learn how not to rely upon my own opinions or the opinions of others. I ask all these things in Jesus's name. Amen.

Declaration of Faith

Today, Lord, I declare that I will trust in You completely, and I will not rely on my own opinions. With all my heart, I declare that I have confidence in You, Heavenly Father, to guide me. I trust You and You alone to lead me in every decision that I make and in the way that I should go.

DAY 2

#iGrace

2 Corinthians 12:9 (NKJV)

And He said to me, "My grace is sufficient for you, for My strength is made perfect in weakness." Therefore most gladly I will rather boast in my infirmities, that the power of Christ may rest upon me.

"His Grace Is Sufficient for Me"

The apostle Paul in this scripture discusses a vision of a thorn in his flesh that led him to persistent prayer for the thorn to be removed. The Word says three times Paul asked the Father to remove the thorn from his flesh. The response Paul received from the Lord was, *"My grace is sufficient for you, for My strength is made perfect in weakness."*

How often do we as believers ask God to remove those hard, seemingly unbearable things from our lives? Things like facing the loss of a job, a home, or finances; the death of a loved one; sickness; or the end of a marriage. We pray, "Lord, please take this or that from me." The pain is so unbearable, and all we want is for it to be gone.

Well, here we learn that God is using the thorn in Paul's flesh to build his spiritual stamina, integrity, and humility—namely, his character. The same is true for us when we find ourselves faced with those *"life happens"* kinds of moments. You might say the Lord allows thorns in our flesh like He did with Paul in order for His glory to be revealed in and through us. God got the glory out of Paul's life. Paul was able to bear the thorn in his flesh because of his persistence in prayer to God. Prayer is our vehicle in the way out of any situation or circumstance we may face.

The Prayer of Faith

Lord, help me when I am faced with difficult situations to humble myself and ask for Your grace to sustain me. Your grace that will sustain me during tests of faith. Lord, reveal to me what it is that You want me to learn from the difficulty that I am facing. Help me to rest in Your grace and to move forward in the things You have called me to do in the ministry of Your kingdom. Strengthen me and uphold me in those areas where I am weak, because it is in the place of my weakness that Your strength is made perfect. Remind me, Lord, that it is in the place of my weakness that I just need to affirm that Your grace and strength is sufficient enough to see me through.

Declaration of Faith

I confess with boldness and confidence in Christ Jesus that "God's grace is sufficient enough for me!"

DAY 3

It Is All for His Glory

Romans 8:18–19 (NKJV)

For I consider that the sufferings of this present time are not worthy to be compared with the glory which shall be revealed in us. For the earnest expectation of the creation eagerly waits for the revealing of the sons of God.

So many times in this life, we find ourselves asking God from our furnace of affliction, "Why me, God? Why is my marriage unstable? Why are my children so far from You? Why does the man of God You told me to marry not love me as Christ loves the church? Why aren't You or why have You not answered my prayers? Why have you not rescued me from this yet? Why do I feel so much rejection even in the ministry? Why must I suffer like this? Why do I feel so alone all the time?"

The "why me" question list becomes endless. It can feel like "I am the only one suffering in this world." But God then brings it all back to focus with this scripture. What a profound message in this verse of His Holy Word. The thought that should be pondered or considered is that the suffering being experienced is nothing compared to the glory of God that will be revealed in me. The idea that all of creation is waiting eagerly for the God in me to be revealed. Pause here and shout, "Hallelujah!" God wants His glory revealed in and through me. That is His desire for me!

Prayer of Faith

God, give me more revelation of Your wisdom, knowledge and understanding about the suffering that I am going through. Give me insight into this suffering so that I come through with greater wisdom, knowledge and understanding not only about the situation, but more importantly about You, LORD. I want more wisdom, knowledge, and understanding of Your nature. My desire is for a closer relationship with You, to be drawn even closer to You.

Declaration of Faith

I decree and declare and stand in agreement with what the Word says in 2 Corinthians 4:17, that our light affliction, which is but for a moment, is working for me a far more exceeding and eternal weight of glory, *I stand on this word in Jesus's Name.*

DAY 4

God with Us

Zephaniah 3:17 (NLT)

For the LORD your God is living among you. He is a mighty savior. He will take delight in you with gladness. With His love, He will calm all your fears. He will rejoice over you with joyful songs.

My Lord, what a revelation of Your love for us. If only we could truly grasp the true revelation of what that means for us. God, Your love for us has such depth and breadth. You love us even when our ability to trust You is not there. You love us when we are drowning in our own doubts and fears. You love us when we make bad choices and decisions. In fact, in many situations, You love us right through them and then restore us back through Your grace so that we are back in right relationship with You. You love us when we are unlovable to others, and even to our own selves. You love us when we do not serve You with our whole hearts.

Prayer of Faith

Father, as Your Word says in this verse, continue to live, dwell, abide, take up residence, have your home, inhabit, and occupy and live with me by Your mighty power. Be with me wherever I find myself today and always. I totally surrender myself to You and You alone. You are indeed the mighty God and our Savior, the one who has all that I could ever want, need, or even desire. Your presence cannot be compared to anyone or anything. Take pleasure in me with Your gladness. Lord, may I experience the continuous filling of Your great love. May Your love never stop being for me. In other words, just don't stop loving me. This is my sincere prayer to You today and always. Continue to dwell with me with Your love and rejoicing over me with Your songs of joy.

Declaration of Faith

I am confident in this: the Lord is with me. He is a mighty warrior fighting all my battles because He is my mighty Savior. I decree and declare that I am loved by a loving Father, and He rejoices over me with songs of joy.

DAY 5

Walk Wisely

Ephesians 5:15–16 (Amplified Bible)

Therefore see that you walk carefully [living life with honor, purpose, and courage; shunning those who tolerate and enable evil], not as the unwise, but as wise [sensible, intelligent, discerning people],]making the very most of your time [on earth, recognizing and taking advantage of each opportunity and using it with wisdom and diligence], because the days are [filled with] evil.

When I read this verse of scripture, the thought that comes to mind is, one who does not walk wisely in the knowledge of God and all that He has for us, this person is a foolish person. As God's own people, we have been called, created by Him with purpose, and filled with His destiny for our lives. It is our responsibility to walk circumspectly, cautiously, vigilantly, carefully, and guardedly before our God as we carry out His plan and purpose for our lives. We must guard our intent, emotions, and attitudes in our interactions with others. God has endowed us with so much authority on earth through His omnipotent power. We are that chosen generation that must walk wisely as His representatives on earth.

Prayer of Faith

Father, Your Word says in Psalms 37 verse 23, *"The steps of a good man are ordered by the LORD."* Your Word then goes on to say in that same chapter, in verse 24, *"Though he fall, he shall not be utterly cast down; for the LORD upholds him with His hand" (NKJV).* Dear Lord, it is my hearts' cry today that You order my steps in Your Word, will, purpose, and plan for my life. For then I can be sure that I am walking in Your wisdom. I know that wisdom, according to your Word in Proverbs 4:7, is *"the principal thing and that I am to get wisdom, and that in all of my getting I am to get understanding."*

Dear God, give me Your understanding. Father God, my desire is to walk heavy in Your wisdom, to make wise, purposeful steps in the way that You would have me to go. So, in the words of an old hymn of the church,

> *Keep Me in Your Pathway LORD /*
> *keep me in the pathway LORD, /*
> *I don't want to stumble,*
> *I don't want to fall, /*
> *keep me in the pathway LORD.*

Declaration of Faith

I decree and declare that I have the mind of Christ. I decree and declare that I walk heavy in the wisdom of the Almighty God. I will fulfill God's purpose and calling for my life by His grace, wisdom, and mercy.

DAY 6

Just Keep on Praying

1 Thessalonians 5:16–18 (NLT)

Always be joyful. Never stop praying. Be thankful in all circumstances, for this is God's will for you who belong to Christ Jesus.

What does it really mean to just keep on praying? No matter what—just keep on praying. Even when it feels like your prayers are hitting a brass ceiling, just keep on praying. Just keep on praying even when there is no immediate answer from God. Just keep on praying when you don't know how to pray. Just keep on praying when you don't feel like praying. Just keep on praying when God has not responded the way you thought He should or when you thought He should have answered by now. Just keep on praying when you fear how God is going to respond. Just keep on praying knowing that whatever situations or difficulties you may face, you can bring them to God in prayer.

God wants us even when our circumstances seem hopeless to rejoice in, knowing that we can just keep on praying. May we be ever so mindful of this scripture and stay in faith knowing that God will answer our prayers with what is best for you and in His own timing. That's a lot to accept! But just keep on praying!

Prayer of Faith

Lord, help me to maintain the posture and the position of being in continual prayer to You no matter what. Lord, help me to keep my heart filled with joy and thankfulness for whatever I may be going through. Help me to see Your hand of mercy lifting me up and guiding me through the process. May I keep the lyrics of the following song by Edna Randolph Worrell in my spirit:

> "Don't stop *praying!*
> *the LORD is nigh;*
> *Don't stop praying!*
> *He'll hear your cry;*
> *God has promised, and He is true;*
> *Don't stop praying;*
> *He'll answer you.'*

Declaration of Faith

I decree and declare that I serve a God who answers my prayer, and I will continue to seek Him with my whole heart. I will never stop praying. I will pray at all times no matter what the situation or circumstance of my life.

DAY 7

Worship the Holy God

Luke 1:46–50 (NLT)

And Mary said: "My soul magnifies the LORD, And my spirit has rejoiced in God my Savior. For He has regarded my lowly state of His maidservant; For behold all generations will call me blessed. For He who is mighty has done great things for me, And holy is His name. And His mercy is on those who fear Him From generation to generation.

Mary's response to the LORD upon learning that she would carry the Christ child in her womb praised Him, acknowledged the greatness of God, the holiness of His name and the mighty power of our God. Mary's expression of praise and exaltation of God reflects adoration, humility, and that of a willing obedience to serve our God. God is so worthy of the praise, honor and the glory of His people. May we all learn from Mary's example here in scripture how to worship our God who is a holy God. Let's worship Him with all of our very being and be willing to surrender all we have to Him.

Prayer of Faith

Lord, may my worship, like the Virgin Mary, when she learned that she was to be the mother of the Christ child, be a sweet sound in Your ear. Like Mary, Lord, I worship You in the beauty and splendor of Your holiness. I worship You as a Holy and righteous God who is altogether lovely. Lord, thank You that You have chosen me to serve in Your kingdom as Your maidservant. Use me, Lord, as You see fit. Lord, I can even ask that You help me to stay in right standing with You. Help me in my weaknesses to be pure and holy, tried and true. You are a great and mighty God. Your mercy toward me is not just for the present generation but for all generations who fear You, reverence You, and acknowledge You as their God.

Declaration of Faith

Lord, this is my declaration of faith to You. You are the great God of this world, and I worship You and You alone. I acknowledge that You are the only true God.

DAY 8

Know God's Plan for Your Life

Jeremiah 29:11–13 (NKJV)

For I know the thoughts that I think towards you, says the LORD, thoughts of peace and not of evil, to give you a future and a hope. Then you will call upon Me and go and pray to Me, and I will listen to you. And you will seek Me and find Me, when you search for Me with all your heart.

God knows His plan for you. The question is, do you know God's plan for your life? We see from these verses of scripture that our God has a plan and purpose for each of our lives. It is time for us to know directly from God His purpose for our lives. Not the purpose or plan we have for our lives but what we were born to do on earth for God. It could very well be a passion that is driving you, pulling you in line with His purpose for your life. I believe that spending time in prayer with Him like the scripture says will lead you right into God's purpose. Prayer is key to us knowing God's purpose for our lives and these scriptures reminds us of that.

Prayer of Faith

Father, my desire is to know Your purpose for my life. Reveal to me, Father, Your purpose and the "ministry call" that You have placed upon my life. Lord, I do not want to waste any more unnecessary time, effort, and money being outside of Your will and purpose for my life. Father, help me to spend time studying Your word and seeking You in prayer for the purpose You have designed for me. Help me to seek You with my whole heart. Help me to be mindful of all hindrances and distractions that prevent me from spending time with You. I thank You in advance for all that will be revealed to me by the Holy Spirit as I spend time praying and studying Your Word. It is in Jesus's name that I pray! Amen.

Declaration of Faith

I believe by faith that the all-knowing God of this world has placed His purpose in me. And I decree that He will make known to me His purpose for my life.

DAY 9

Be an Obedient Servant

Isaiah 50:4–5 (KJV)

The Lord GOD hath given me the tongue of the learned, that I should know how to speak a word in season, to him that is weary: he wakeneth morning by morning, he wakeneth mine ear to hear as the learned. The Lord GOD hath opened mine ear, and I was not rebellious, neither turned away back.

As I read and meditate upon this scripture, I realize that I serve a God who is willing to make me smart, ready, well prepared to follow His leading, and to walk in the way He has prepared for me each day in the service of His people. Applying the principles of this scripture, which is to seek Him early in the morning for direction, prepares us for how we can effectively minister to His people and people of the world. It is God's desire, I believe, that we at the very beginning of each day be in alignment with His plan for us. By doing this we cannot fail at anything we set our hands to do. Making the decision to do this for ourselves also puts us in position to teach and serve those we encounter.

Prayer of Faith

Lord, Your word says that you have given me the tongue of the learned which indicates that I am well equipped to administer Your knowledge to Your people. Lord, this also means as one of your people with a learned tongue that I have been given authority by You to instruct Your people at the right time in their lives about situations and circumstances in their lives. May I be very attuned to hearing Your instructions for Your people. May Your anointing rest upon my ears for the responsibility that You have placed upon me. Give me the ability also to impart Your instruction with the love and compassion that is so characteristic of Your nature.

Declaration of Faith

Father, I will hear and obey Your voice as one who possesses a learned tongue given by You!

DAY 10

There Was No King Like Josiah

2 Kings 23:25 (NIRV)

There was no king like Josiah before or after him. None of them turned to the LORD as he did. He followed the LORD with all his heart and all his soul. He followed him with all his strength. He did everything the Law of Moses required.

Josiah, according to Bible scholars who wrote the Life Application Bible, is remembered as Judah's most obedient King. This Old Testament scripture serves as a great reminder of how we as God's people should follow Him. The Word of God here says that King Josiah followed God with his whole heart and all his soul.

What exactly does that mean? It means that being one who is a follower of God, you must be totally sold out to the will of God for your life. One who is truly willing to do whatever God is leading or directing you to do by the power of the Holy Spirit. Likewise, a true follower of Christ will shun sin and evil and live a life of righteousness that is a true witness of the love of Christ. This can only be done by obeying God's Word and being led by the Holy Spirit. Because apart from God, we cannot do this.

Prayer of Faith

Father, give me the heart of following hard after you like King Josiah did, as it says in 2 Kings 23:25, the scripture for today. My hearts cry today is to be more like You and less like what the world says I should be. I want to be a good ambassador and witness of You in this world. Help me to be mindful of things that would draw me away from You and Your Word. Thank You for the gift of the Holy Spirit that helps me in all that I do to remain faithful to You and You alone.

Declaration of Faith

I am created in the likeness and image of God. I have the mind of Christ. Therefore, by the power of Holy Spirit that resides in me, I will live in such a manner that reflects that I am God's representative in the earth!

DAY 11

"Just Git Err Done"

Ecclesiastes 9:8–10 (NIV)

Always be clothed in white, and always anoint your head with oil. Enjoy life with your wife, whom you love, all the days of this meaningless life that God has given you under the sun—all your meaningless days. For this is your lot in life and in your toilsome labor under the sun. Whatever your hand finds to do, do it with all your might, for in the realm of the dead, where you are going, there is neither working nor planning nor knowledge nor wisdom.

Solomon in this passage of scripture is speaking to his son about the uncertainty of life. Truly we do not know what the future holds for us. But as I have heard many of the older saints say, "But I know the man who holds the future." That man is God. Solomon is encouraging his son to enjoy life. Life has a way of bringing moments that rob us of joy, so get what Solomon is saying to his son about enjoying life. We also see in this passage the importance of getting things done with all of our might. Why? Because it would be unfortunate to carry the things that God has ordained or predestined for us to do to our graves. Someone needs that God idea for a book, someone needs to see after the least, the lost, the left behind and disenfranchised, or that God idea for ministry. These are just some of the things God has placed us here on earth to do. *So "just git err done"!*

Prayer of Faith

Heavenly Father, as I meditate upon this Word today from the book of Ecclesiastes, enlighten my understanding by the power of the Holy Spirit. Help me to understand the importance of not only enjoying each day that You have given as a gift but to also be busy about doing Your business on Earth. Help me to put Your business first and to do Your business with all my might. Help me to stop wasting time.

Declaration of Faith

I decree and declare that by the power of the Holy Spirit working in me, *"I can do all things through Christ who strengtheneth me"* (Phil. 4:13, KJV). Hallelujah!

DAY 12

Do Not Get So Big and Forget God

Deuteronomy 8:12–18 (NIV)

When you have eaten and are full, and have built beautiful houses and dwell in them; and when your herds and your flocks multiply, and your silver and your gold are multiplied, and all that you have is multiplied; when your heart is lifted up, and you forget the LORD your God who brought you out of the land of Egypt, from the house of bondage; who led you through that great and terrible wilderness, in which were fiery serpents and scorpions and thirsty land where there was no water; who brought water for you out of the flinty rock; who fed you in the wilderness with manna, which your fathers did not know, that He might humble you and that He might test you, to do you good in the end—then you say in your heart, 'My power and the might of my hand have gained me this wealth.' "And you shall remember the LORD your God, for it is He who gives you power to get wealth, that He may establish His covenant which He swore to your fathers, as it is this day.

For us followers of Christ, it can be very easy to forget God when we achieve great success in our lives, as the writer of Deuteronomy is warning against in these verses. He is reminding the Israelites that God delivered them from the hand of the Egyptian taskmaster. We are often quick to boast that our success is the result of hard work and knowing how to work your plan for success. These moments of success and triumph can also be a distraction luring us away from the things of God. Before we know it, we start to spend less time with God in prayer, our church attendance gets neglected, reading His Word, and reflecting upon the goodness of our God is a thing of the past. The Israelites are being warned here not to succumb to forgetting God and His goodness to them. God deserves the credit for all greatness that we achieve in this life.

Prayer of Faith

LORD, today I approach You with a humble heart of thanksgiving and praise for all that You have done for me. Thank You for making sure that every need is met in my life. I used to hear my grandparents say it this way in prayer, "Thank you for life's welfare just as it is." When I hear those particular words in my spirit from their prayers from the past, I think they were thanking You, God, for all things great and small, good or bad. So, I, like my ancestors, just want to thank You, LORD. Thank you for all things, God. Thank You for Your goodness, grace, and mercy; and thank you for releasing to me Your power and ability to get wealth and achieve success.

Declaration of Faith

Father, I will continue to trust You and give You all the praise, glory, and honor for any and all things that I am able to achieve in this life. You deserve all of the praise!

Glory to God!

DAY 13

There Is God, Who Knows All About Me

Psalm 139:1–6 (NKJV)

O LORD, You have searched me and known me. You know my sitting down and my rising up; You understand my thought afar off. You comprehend my path and my lying down, And are acquainted with all my ways. For there is not a word on my tongue, But behold, O LORD, You know it altogether. You have hedged me behind and before, And laid Your hand upon me. Such knowledge is too wonderful for me; It is high, I cannot attain it.

Only a perfect God can know your thoughts. Only a perfect and loving Father would even care to know Your thoughts. Only a perfect and faithful Father is willing to be with you through every situation or circumstance you face. Only a perfect Father protects you from dangers seen and unseen. What a mighty God He is, and who would not want a relationship with a God like Jehovah. For there is no other God like Jehovah!

Prayer of Faith

Lord, my prayer is that You daily search my heart as Your Word says in Psalm 139 to ensure that I am in fellowship with You, that I have a heart that is free from sin and in right standing with You, that I am in Your will for my life, that I remain in Your path for my life, and that I live and lead a life in constant unity with You. For who knows me better than You, the God who is omniscient. Thank You, Father, for being with me at all times.

Declaration of Faith

I declare that I am a follower of Christ who knows me better than anyone in the world and beyond. He is my Lord, my Savior, and my God. I surrender my all—heart, mind, body soul, and spirit to the God who is omniscient-all knowing, omnipotent-all powerful and omnipresent-always with me.

Glory to God who reigns forever and ever!

DAY 14

Full Joy and Pleasures of God Forevermore

Psalms 16:8–11 (RSV)

I keep the LORD always before me; because he is at my right hand, I shall not be moved. Therefore my heart is glad, and my soul rejoices; my body also dwells secure. For thou dost not give me up to Sheol, or let thy godly one see the Pit. Thou dost show me the path of life; in thy presence there is fulness of joy, in thy right hand are pleasures forevermore.

As we advance forward in our *next* move in God, it is the presence of God and the power of God's right hand that is so very much needed. We see here in the Word of God that the Psalmist acknowledges that he keeps the Lord ever before him because it is there that he finds the *right hand of God*. We learn further in Psalms 16:11, where the Word says, "You, make known to me the path of life, You, will fill me with Your presence, with eternal pleasures at Your right hand" that there are three benefits in God's presence.

The *first* is that He will show us His path, the *second,* is that in God's presence, we find fullness of joy, and *finally*, at God's right hand are pleasures forevermore. Meditate upon this word and allow it to minister to you.

Prayer of Faith

Father, my heart's cry is for more of You and less of me and the things of this world. May I find myself always in Your presence where I have the benefits of Your showing and keeping me on the path You set for my life, Your fullness of joy and pleasure forevermore in Your righteous right hand. Father, I will praise Your name in all the earth and give You all the glory, honor, and praise.

Declaration of Faith

You are God and God alone, and in Your presence is where I always want to be found. I speak Your Word out loud today from Psalms 16, that You do show me the path of life, that in Your presence is where I will find fullness of joy and Your right hand possesses pleasures forevermore.

DAY 15

Wisdom

Proverbs 1:5 (NKJV)

*A wise man will hear and increase learning,
And a man of understanding will attain wise counsel,*

When you read this passage of scripture, you might ask, why would you not want to grow in learning and receive the wise counsel of God? Yet we see this so much in people today, even the people of God. By now we should not want to be without the wise counsel of God. The wise counsel of God will not allow us to be led astray from God into sin. It causes us to grow in knowledge and understanding.

Prayer of Faith

Lord, give me a tongue that always speaks words of wisdom to those in need of comfort from the cares of life. It seems that the cares of life are weighing Your people down and causing all kinds of despair and feelings of hopelessness. Father, my desire is to be Your audible voice to Your people, speaking words that are rich in encouragement and that come from You. Life-sustaining words. Awaken me, Lord, each morning and open my ears to hear from You. I want to be Your mouth on earth that speaks encouragement to Your people.

Declaration of Faith

Lord, I decree that I have a mind that is in perfect peace because my mind is focused on You. I can make this declaration based on Your Word in Isaiah 26, because I trust You, Jehovah God. Therefore, I can speak with boldness what You want expressed to not only Your people, but to all people.

DAY 16

God, Give Us Wisdom for Prosperity

Deuteronomy 8:18 (AMP Bible)

But you shall remember [with profound respect] the LORD your God, for it is He who is giving you power to make wealth, that He may confirm His covenant which He swore (solemnly promised) to your fathers, as it is this day.

God, help me to understand the question you downloaded in my spirit. Why does God want me to pray for the wisdom for prosperity? I think the answer is connected to His Word in Deuteronomy 8:18. LORD, help me to understand what Your Word says in Deuteronomy 8:18. Simply stated here, the Word of God is saying that it is God who gives us the power to get wealth. Wealth that is not just financial wealth but an all-inclusive wealth. God wants us to prosper not just in financial wealth but in the riches of His grace, His wisdom, His mercy, His compassion His glory, and His great love for us.

Proverbs 10:22 in the Amplified Bible says it this way: *"The blessing of the LORD brings [true] riches, And He adds no sorrow to it [for it comes as a blessing from God]. So bless us LORD and make us to prosper in every aspect of life!"*

Prayer of Faith

O God, give me the wisdom for prosperity. You said in Your Word that I could ask, and so just as it says in James 1:5, *"If any of you lacks wisdom, you should ask God, who gives generously to all without finding fault, and it will be given to you.* So I boldly ask, O God, give me wisdom for prosperity. God, I believe that it is your will for me to be prosperous based on your word in 3 John 2, so I pray, according to your word, *"that in all respects that I may prosper and be in health, just as my soul prospers."* Grant me the wisdom to do so. Show me how to prosper in every aspect of my life, in my relationship with You, my health, my wealth, my marriage, and in my family.

Declaration of Faith

I decree and declare, according to Your Word in Deuteronomy 1:11, (paraphrased) that the Lord, the God of *our* fathers, will increase *me* a thousand-fold more than I am and bless *me*, just as He has promised *me*!

"May the Lord, the God of your fathers, increase you a thousand-fold more than you are and bless you, just as He has promised you!" (NASB)

DAY 17

Nehemiah's Prayer for a Nation

Nehemiah 1:5–10 (NIV)

Then I said: "Lord, the God of heaven, the great and awesome God, who keeps his covenant of love with those who love him and keep his commandments, let your ear be attentive and your eyes open to hear the prayer your servant is praying before you day and night for your servants, the people of Israel. I confess the sins we Israelites, including myself and my father's family, have committed against you. We have acted very wickedly toward you. We have not obeyed the commands, decrees and laws you gave your servant Moses.

"Remember the instruction you gave your servant Moses, saying, 'If you are unfaithful, I will scatter you among the nations, but if you return to me and obey my commands, then even if your exiled people are at the farthest horizon, I will gather them from there and bring them to the place I have chosen as a dwelling for my Name.'

"They are your servants and your people, whom you redeemed by your great strength and your mighty hand. Lord, let your ear be attentive to the prayer of this your servant and to the prayer of your servants who delight in revering your name. Give your servant success today by granting him favor in the presence of this man."

Nehemiah was Cupbearer to the King

We find in chapter 1, in the book of Nehemiah, one of the most powerful prayers in the Bible about a nation whose walls were in ruin and the need for rebuilding those walls. It also appears in chapter 1 that the burden for the rebuilding of the walls in Jerusalem fell upon the heart of Nehemiah.

Because upon hearing about the conditions of the walls in Jerusalem as well as the remnant of Jews who were there in exile, Nehemiah sought the Lord through fasting and prayer. Nehemiah's prayer serves as an example to us of how to respond when we are faced with a crisis or crises in our lives. This prayer is a model of a man's humility to a great God. It is an example of a man's willingness to acknowledge the sin of a nation of people and the need for the grace and mercy of Almighty God. What an awesome prayer example for us today.

Are there walls in our lives that need rebuilding? Walls of hurt frustration, hurt, disappointment, rejection, or discouragement. Build us up, O Lord, as only you can. We bring our prayers and fasting to you as a sacrifice to You and You alone.

Prayer of Faith

LORD as a people and as a Nation we have sinned against You and You alone by not acknowledging that You are a great and mighty God worthy of all honor, praise and glory. You love us with an everlasting love and You care for us in every way. LORD, You, provide for us in such an awesome way. Thank You for being so gracious towards us even when we are not always deserving of Your love and generosity. LORD, thank You for Your loving kindness and faithfulness. LORD, I offer the prayer of the Nehemiah to You on behalf of our Nation.

Declaration of Faith

So, Lord, after praying the prayer of Nehemiah, I declare, according to James 5:16 (KJV), *"the effectual fervent prayer of a righteous man availeth much."*

DAY 18

By My Spirit

Zechariah 4:6 (ESV)

Then he said to me, "This is the word of Zerubbabel: Not by might, nor by power, but by my Spirit, says the LORD of hosts."

As God's chosen people, many of us are called to some very challenging tasks. Some challenging tasks include addressing social injustices like human sex trafficking, helping people seeking refuge in the United States, and establishing kingdom ministries for the homeless and the abused. These tasks are to be fulfilled for the Kingdom of God. The word from Zechariah is one of encouragement to the Israelites, who had returned to Jerusalem after being in exile. Zechariah encourages Zerubbabel, the one with the responsibility of rebuilding the temple in Jerusalem, to not attempt to do this in his own power and might. May we gain momentum and encouragement with the challenges we face with our calling from the words of the prophet Zechariah to Zerubbabel. Zerubbabel was anointed by God's Spirit to get the job done, and so are we. For it is through God's Spirit that we will be able accomplish lasting things for Him.

Prayer of Faith

Heavenly Father, help me to realize that it is only by Your Spirit that I am able to accomplish any work for Your kingdom as well as ourselves.

I need your leading, guidance, and counsel to get the work of Your kingdom done. My desire is to see Your glory operating in my ministry, business, and establishments. Lord, it is all for Your glory. Lord, I value Your anointing and realize my success will only be accomplished through that anointing. So, Heavenly Father, may Your anointing remain upon me for all that I have to do for Your kingdom as well as for others. I am truly are about conducting Kingdom business for Your glory. I praise You and honor You for the blessing of Your anointing.

Declaration of Faith

Heavenly Father, it is not by my power nor is it by my might that I am able to do anything. It is only by Your Spirit that I am able to do anything. I decree and declare that I am completely dependent on Your strength, and I operate in the spirit of Your power.

DAY 19

We Fight in the Power of His Might

Ephesians 6:12–13 (NKJV)

For we do not wrestle against flesh and blood, but against principalities, against powers, against the rulers of the darkness of this age, against spiritual hosts of wickedness in the heavenly places. Therefore take up the whole armor of God, that you may be able to withstand in the evil day, and having done all, to stand.

As believers, we realize that our fight is not against flesh and blood but is that of a spiritual nature. We can no longer enter the fight seeing it from a natural or physical perspective. Because the fight is spiritual, we must come to the fight fully prepared to do battle being fully dressed for the fight with the full armor of God.

Prayer of Faith

Father, help me to dress for the fight according to Your Word in Ephesians chapter 6. Help me to come to the fight ready to stand firm with the *belt of truth* around my waist. Strengthen me with having the *breastplate of righteousness* in place. May *my feet* be fitted and ready to spread the gospel of peace. Then there is the need for me, Father, to take up the *shield of faith*. Upon my head I will have the *helmet of salvation*. And finally, Father, help me to remember to come with the sword of the Spirit, which is the Word of God. Help me to always be battle ready praying in the Spirit on all occasions with all kinds of prayers. (Right now, right where you are as you are reading this devotional, begin to pray in the Spirit.) I know that dressing myself for spiritual battle and praying in this manner is a game changer for the enemy. For being clothed and praying in the Spirit gives me the victory over all enemy forces. Amen!

Declaration of Faith

I have the victory over the forces of the enemy because I am dressed in the full armor of God, and I pray in the Spirit on all occasions! I seal this declaration with the blood of Jesus. Battle ready in Jesus's mighty name.

DAY 20

Prayer of Faith and Strength for the Church

Ephesians 3:14–19 (NKJV)

For this reason I bow my knees to the Father of our Lord Jesus Christ, from whom the whole family in heaven and earth is named, that He would grant you, according to the riches of His glory, to be strengthened with might through His Spirit in the inner man, that Christ may dwell in your hearts through faith; that you, being rooted and grounded in love, may be able to comprehend with all the saints what is the width and length and depth and height—to know the love of Christ which passes knowledge; that you may be filled with all the fullness of God.

We see here that the man of God, namely, Paul, provides a great example of how we are to pray for each other. In this prayer, we see Paul's love and compassion for God and God's people. Paul's humility to God is also demonstrated here as he takes the position in prayer of being on bended knees before our Lord and Savior, the Lord Jesus Christ. Paul encourages the people of God to be strengthened in the power of and their faith in God.

Prayer of Faith

Lord, thank you for this prayer that demonstrates Your love for the church. Paul really captured the heart of Your people in this prayer.

Lord, I need so much at times to be strengthened in my inner self by Your precious Spirit. Help me to be so deeply rooted and grounded in Your Word. Reveal more of Your nature and character to me as I study and meditate upon Your Word.

Lord, give me a mind that is overflowing with the knowledge of You. Lord, thank you for your love that gives me full access to You. Access that enables me to be filled with the fullness of You, God.

Declaration of Faith

Because I am being rooted and grounded in love, I have the mind of God. I think like God. I am filled with the fullness of God.

DAY 21

His Peace Keeps Me

Isaiah 26:3–4 (NJKV)

You will keep him in perfect peace, Whose mind is stayed on You, Because he trusts in You. Trust in the LORD forever, For in YAH, the LORD, is everlasting strength.

As believers, we often find ourselves living in situations and circumstances of uncertainties. We are not sure if God is going to heal our bodies, we are not sure we will have the resources needed for our retirement, or what if I will not be able to fulfill the call of God in my life. What does the future really hold for me? The uncertainties often leave us feeling anxious and unsettled in our minds. Our thoughts can lead us to a place of negativity, to the point we find it difficult to center our thoughts on *"whatever things are true, whatever things are noble, whatever things are just, whatever things are pure, whatever things are lovely, whatever things are of good report, if there is any virtue and if there is anything praiseworthy—meditate on these things"* (NKJV). It is at this point that we need the peace of God.

Prayer of Faith

Lord, I choose to pray and stand on your Word in Isaiah 26 today. I need for my mind to be in your perfect peace. I need my trust in You to be fortified in my mind. So, Lord, I am asking that thoughts of trust in

You overtake me. I need the strength of Your power and might to even trust You. You are a gracious God, and Your mercy is life sustaining. Give me that peace that allows me to think like the scripture says in Philippians 4. I choose to think on things that are "true, pure and noble, lovely, and of good report." These things will I meditate upon.

Declaration of Faith

I boldly confess that God keeps my mind in perfect peace because I trust God. Because I trust You, God, my mind is in perfect peace. I trust God with the peace of my mind.

DAY 22

So, Whose Report Do You Believe?

Isaiah 53:1–3 (NKJV)

Who has believed our report? And to whom has the arm of the LORD been revealed?

For He shall grow up before Him as a tender plant, And as a root out of dry ground.

He has no form or comeliness; And when we see Him, There is no beauty that we should desire Him. He is despised and rejected by men, A Man of sorrows and acquainted with grief. And we hid, as it were, our faces from Him; He was despised, and we did not esteem Him.

We are living in a time and in a world where there is much confusion about whom to believe and what to believe. It seems that the world has truly lost sight of real truth. Which brings us to the question of, what is the real truth and the source of that truth?

I believe the answer is God and His Word, the Bible. The Bible is full of God's Knowledge, God's Truth, God's Wisdom and Revelation about Himself, and anything you could or would possibly need to know. So to help us reset our minds and thoughts on the real truth, I want to remind all of us whose report we can believe. We do not have to ponder this question any longer because Jesus Christ came as God's representative on earth and left us with the knowledge of Himself in His Word. His coming was prophesied in these verses of scripture.

The account of the Messiah's coming as prophesied by the prophet Isaiah is found in John chapter 12:37–41 (NKJV).

Who Has Believed Our Report?

But although He had done so many signs before them, they did not believe in Him, that the word of Isaiah the prophet might be fulfilled, which he spoke:

"Lord, who has believed our report? And to whom has the arm of the LORD been revealed?" Therefore they could not believe, because Isaiah said again: "He has blinded their eyes and hardened their hearts, Lest they should see with their eyes, Lest they should understand with their hearts and turn, So that I should heal them."

These things Isaiah said when he saw His glory and spoke of Him.

Jesus had performed many miracles at that time, and people still did not believe Him. The same is true today despite all that God does for us and what we know about Him. Many times, we still have difficulty believing that God will see us through those difficult and often-challenging times.

Prayer of Faith

Lord, in times of being tested in my faith, help me to go to Your Word and stand on Your promises. When I am weak in my faith and the accuser comes, help me to remind the accuser who I am in You. Help me to say with confidence and boldness, "I am the redeemed of the LORD, and I say so."

This writer loves how the people of God at Lakewood Church confess not only their belief in You, but also their belief in the Bible and its transforming power in their lives. Lord, allow my faith to increase as I study and meditate on Your Word daily. Help me to see the importance of living my life on the basis of Your Word and making it applicable to my life. Lord, thank you for your Word and the freedom I have to worship You. Amen!

Declaration of Faith

In the words of the Lakewood Church confession, I decree and declare the following:

> This is my Bible. I am what it says I am, I have what it says I have, I can do what it says I can do. Today, I will be taught the word of God. I boldly confess: My mind is alert, my heart is receptive, I will never be the same, in Jesus' name! Amen. (JoelOsteen.com)

DAY 23

Why We Can Believe the Report of the Lord

Who can believe the report of the Lord? The answer to the question posed by the prophet Isaiah (from our previous reading) and then later raised again in John after the Messiah came is this: We can believe the report of the Lord. The Bible contains God's report. His Word is true, and all that is required of us is that we have faith and believe in His Word.

Romans 10:9 says, *"If you confess with your mouth the Lord Jesus and believe in your heart that God has raised Him from the dead, you will be saved. For with the heart one believes unto righteousness, and with the mouth confession is made unto salvation."*

So let's choose today to believe the report of the Lord. Let's reset our minds to believe the report of the Lord based on the promises found in His Word.

Prayer of Faith

Please read, meditate, and pray the following scriptures related to the "report of the LORD, from the Bible," that I have included in the Declarations of Faith for today. Start here by praying the following:

Father I pray and believe the Word of the LORD when it says that You are my Shepard and that You watch over me because the Bible says the following in Psalm 23 (KJV):

The LORD is my shepherd; I shall not want. He maketh me to lie down in green pastures: He leadeth me beside the still waters. He restoreth my soul: He leadeth me in the paths of righteousness for His name's sake. Yea, though I walk through the valley of the shadow of death, I will fear no evil: for thou art with me; thy rod and thy staff they comfort me. Thou preparest a table before me in the presence of mine enemies: thou anointest my head with oil; my cup runneth over. Surely goodness and mercy shall follow me all the days of my life: and I will dwell in the house of the LORD forever.

Declarations of Faith

I can believe the report of the Lord concerning God's love and my salvation because the Bible reports in John 3:16, *"For God so loved the world that He gave His only begotten Son, that whoever believes in Him should not perish but have everlasting life. For God did not send His Son into the world to condemn the world, but that the world through Him might be saved."*

I can believe the report of the Lord concerning my strength in Him because the Bible reports in Philippians 4:13, that *"I can do all things through Christ who strengthens me."*

I can believe that God will provide for me because the Bible reports in the book of Philippians 4:19, *"And my God shall supply all your need according to His riches in glory by Christ Jesus."*

I can believe that God wants us to prosper and be in good health because the Bible reports in 3 John, *"Beloved, I pray that you may prosper in all things and be in health, just as your soul prospers."*

As a Christ follower and Believer I can believe that with God all things are possible because the Bible reports in Luke 18:27, *"The things which are impossible with men are possible with God."*

I can believe that God will help me when I am in trouble because the Bible reports in Psalms 46:1 that *"God is our refuge and strength, a very present help in trouble."*

The Bible reports in Romans 8:28, *"And we know that all things work together for good to those who love God, to those who are the called according to His purpose. I just need to believe this truth from God's word.*

I can believe that God is not a liar because the Word of God in Numbers 23:19 assures me that *"God is not a man, that He should lie, Nor a son of man, that He should repent. Has He said, and will He not do? Or has He spoken, and will He not make it good?*

DAY 24

I Give You Jesus

Acts 3:1–10 (AMP)

Healing the Lame Beggar

Now Peter and John were going up to the temple at the hour of prayer, the ninth hour (3:00 p.m.), and a man who had been unable to walk from birth was being carried along, whom they used to set down every day at that gate of the temple which is called Beautiful, so that he could beg alms from those entering the temple. So when he saw Peter and John about to go into the temple, he began asking [them] for coins. But Peter, along with John, stared at him intently and said, "Look at us!" And the man began to pay attention to them, eagerly expecting to receive something from them. But Peter said, "Silver and gold I do not have; but what I do have I give to you: In the name (authority, power) of Jesus Christ the Nazarene—[begin now to] walk and go on walking!" Then he seized the man's right hand with a firm grip and raised him up. And at once his feet and ankles became strong and steady, and with a leap he stood up and began to walk; and he went into the temple with them, walking and leaping and praising God. All the people saw him walking and praising God; and they recognized him as the very man who usually sat begging for coins at the Beautiful Gate of the temple, and they were filled with wonder and amazement and were mystified at what had happened to him.

The encounter of the Lame Beggar by Peter and John as they were entering the temple to offer prayers, as was their custom, that day left the Beggar with more than he asked for. That encounter proved to be a life changer for him. Not only did he receive healing that day, but he was given the power and authority of Almighty God. When we read the account of the situation with the Lame Beggar, let us reflect upon what we have gained as a result of accepting Jesus as our Savior. We too have been given access to the power and authority of the Almighty God.

Prayer of Faith

Father, I thank You for giving me Your only begotten Son, Jesus. I thank You, Father God, for giving me Jesus who is my Redeemer, my peace, my joy, and my hope. Father, I thank You for giving me Jesus, who took on the sins for all the world. Thank You for giving me Jesus who is my Healer and my Provider. Thank You, God, for giving me Jesus who is a comforter to me. Thank You, God, for giving me Jesus who is the Great Shepherd over me. Father, thank You for giving me Jesus who is the greatest friend anyone could ever have. Thank You, God, for giving me Jesus!

Declaration of Faith

I decree and declare that Jesus is LORD over my life.

DAY 25

God Wants the Best for Us

3 John 2 (NASB)

Beloved, I pray that in all respects you may prosper and be in good health, just as your soul prospers.

Isn't it good to know that the Lord loves us so much that He Himself prays for our well-being and prosperity? That He is concerned about not just our souls but our bodies too? As you read and meditate upon this word, let this concern that the Lord has for us really take root in our thoughts to the point that we desire to take care of our health better. It is so important that we take responsibility for maintaining good physical health and discipline ourselves to not indulge in unhealthy behaviors that impact our bodies. God wants us healthy so that we are at our best in His service.

Prayer of Faith

Father, thank You, that Your love for me is that I prosper and be in good health. Your desire is that all may go well for me, even as my soul is being prospered. Lord, thank You for this prayer and how in this prayer I am able to experience and feel the love and compassion that you have for my personal health and well-being. May this prayer serve as a constant reminder to me of just how important I am to You. In this prayer, I am assured that You really are concerned about me and the things that concern me. The sincerity of Your heart for me is overwhelming. Thank You, Heavenly Father, for this blessing in this Your prayer for me.

Declaration of Faith

I decree and declare that I walk in good health and prosperity in my soul because this is my Heavenly Father's desire for me. I walk in the good things that God has for me. Divine physical health and prosperity are mine. My mind is in good health because my thoughts are of peace and centered on God. I have the confidence of God for these things.

DAY 26

God Wants to Increase You More

Psalm 115:14–15 (KJV)

The LORD shall increase you more and more, you and your children. Ye are blessed of the LORD which made heaven and earth.

This Old Testament scripture is filled with a blessing for abundance from God. When God says that He wants to increase us more and more, what is the increase He is talking about? The Matthew Henry Bible Commentary suggests that the increase here is referring to increase in *knowledge, wisdom, grace, holiness, and joy.* As we meditate upon this scripture and the related commentary, let's begin to see that abundance is not always related to our finances or wealth. That the blessing of more and more means that we have greater access to the wisdom and knowledge of God. May we come to realize that God has blessed us with more of His unearned, undeserved and unmerited grace. May we know and understand that we are only holy and sanctified because of Him. And finally, we have joy because as it says in Nehemiah 8:10b, *"The joy of the LORD is our strength!"*

Prayer of Faith

Father, according to Your Word in Colossians 1:9–14 (the Voice Translation), I humbly pray the following paraphrased prayer asking for knowledge and insight that can only come from You:

Father, may *I* clearly know Your will and achieve *the height and depth of* spiritual wisdom and understanding. May *my life* be a credit to You, Lord; and *what's more,* may *I* continue to delight You by doing every good work and growing in the true knowledge that comes from being close to You. Strengthen *me* with Your infinite power, according to Your glorious might, so that *I* will have everything *I* need to hold on and endure hardship patiently and joyfully. Thank You, Father, as You have made me[a] eligible to receive my portion of the inheritance given to all those set apart by the light. You have rescued me from dark powers and brought me safely into the kingdom of Your Son, whom You love and in whom I am redeemed and forgiven of my sins [through His blood]. Amen!

Declaration of Faith

God has increased me more and more in His knowledge, His wisdom, His grace, His holiness, and His joy! Therefore, I boldly confess, I am increased in knowledge. I am increased in wisdom. I am increased in grace. I am increased in holiness. I am increased in joy. In all of these things, I am increased more and more—me and my children.

DAY 27

To Know Him

Psalm 83:18 (KJV)

That men may know that thou, whose name alone is JEHOVAH, art the most high over all the earth.

In this Psalm, it appears that the writer is offering a prayer to God about his enemies, asking Him to show them just who He is. Sometimes when going going through attacks from the enemy, we want God to expose our enemies to the point of being shamed. I have often asked God to just take them out. But I have come to realize that what is more impactful is for God to really show them just who He is, exercising His power, might, and authority to the point that they realize, like our scripture for the today is saying, that He is the *"most high over all the earth."* His name is Jehovah, which means "Lord and Master."

Prayer of Faith

Father, You, are Jehovah, the God who made the heavens and the earth according to Your Word in Genesis 2:4. I worship You, God, as the only true God, and You are worthy of all of our praises. Father, I acknowledge that even though You rule over all the earth, You, still desire to have relationship with me. What a privilege and honor to serve a God that desires to be in a relationship with me. It is also a privilege and honor to know that I have direct access to You. Jehovah, I am indeed grateful for Your desire to be close to me. Praise the Lord!

Declaration of Faith

Jehovah, You, are the most High God! Jehovah, there is no other God greater than You. Jehovah, You, are all mighty and all powerful. Jehovah, You are the only wise God. Jehovah, You are God over the earth and all creation.

DAY 28

Do You Know What God Has Planned for You?

Jeremiah 29:11–13 (NKJV)

Jeremiah's Letter to the Captives

For I know the thoughts that I think toward you, says the Lord, thoughts of peace and not of evil, to give you a future and a hope. Then you will call upon Me and go and pray to Me, and I will listen to you. And you will seek Me and find Me, when you search for Me with all your heart.

Every one of us as born-again believers in Jesus have a call in our lives that is to be used for building God's kingdom on earth. It would be unfortunate for us, but more so to God, if we did not fulfill God's plan for our lives here on earth. I know for me that I have missed opportunities to move forward in the plan God has for my life. God's plan for my life has been grossly neglected by me, largely because of fear, lack of trust in God, and doubt in my ability to achieve anything useful to God. I have found it very difficult to rely solely on God, or to trust that God has a plan for me. But if I am brutally honest with myself, I gave up on God having a plan for my life and stopped pursuing Him for it because of the reasons mentioned.

I did have some help with stopping my pursuit of God for His plan for my life. The help with calling a halt to pursuing God for the call came in the form of setbacks, rejection, and disappointments. Do not let this be you. I have begun to pursue God again for His plan for me. I have come to believe after having it drilled down to me that it is not too late to pursue Him for His plan for my life.

Prayer of Faith

Father, first of all, please forgive me for giving up on You and Your plan for my life. Father, my desire is to be filled with the knowledge of Your will, plan, and purpose for my life. I ask, Father, that I be filled by You with all wisdom and spiritual understanding. Reveal to me, Father, Your purpose and ministry call for my life. Father, help me to walk worthy of You and the ministry call that is upon my life. Lord, I want to be pleasing to You and fruitful in all that I do for You. My honest and sincere desire is to grow in the knowledge of You, O God. I believe that it is only by increasing in my knowledge of You that I will find Your purpose for my life. More knowledge of You can only be achieved by spending time in Your presence and in Your Word. I believe that as I discipline myself to spend time with You, in prayer, studying Your Word and seeking You with my whole heart, I will find You. And You will make known to me Your plan. Father, I thank You in advance for all that will be revealed to me by the Holy Spirit as I spend time in prayer and studying Your Word. It is in Jesus's name that I pray. Amen!

Declaration of Faith

I believe that the Lord has a plan for my life. Only God possesses the perfect plan for my life. I choose to surrender my will and plans for my life in exchange for God's will and plan for my life. I will no longer halfheartedly pursue God for what He wants to do with my life. Lord, not my will for my life but Your will be done in my life!

DAY 29

I Will Follow God's Plan

Psalm 25:4–5 (TPT)

Lord, direct me throughout my journey so I can experience your plans for my life. Reveal the life-paths that are pleasing to you.

Escort me along the way; take me by the hand and teach me.

For you are the God of my increasing salvation; I have wrapped my heart into yours!

When I mediate upon this scripture, I am reminded of just how important it is to be in lockstep with God's plan and vision for my life. We learned in the previous message that God has a plan for our lives. Now it is time for us to hunker down and spend time in prayer asking Him for His plan, purpose, and vision for the ministry call for your life. Go back and pray the prayer from the previous day. Add to that prayer whatever the Holy Spirit prompts you to pray over yourself concerning your ministry call. Remember that it is important to God that you to fulfill your call for the building of His kingdom here on earth while you are here. As you spend time in the presence of God pray this prayer from the words of Dr. M. L. King Jr.: "God, help us to believe we were created for that which is noble and good; help us to live in the light of Your great calling and destiny." Now ask God to help you write the vision for the ministry He has given you.

Prayer of Faith

Father, help me to spend good, quality time in Your Presence and in Your Word. Holy Spirit of God, strengthen me in this area of my life. Show me the areas of my life that need more self-discipline when it comes to spending time in Your presence and in Your Word. Hear this my prayer about this matter, Father, and help me! Father, God, it so important for me to learn how to seek You in prayer for better clarity, wisdom, understanding, and for my total surrender to the leadership of Jesus.

Declaration of Faith

I have been called by God to do great things for His Kingdom to be glorified on earth. I am destined by God to do great things for Him. "I can do all things through Christ who strengthens me."

"All things are possible with God" to include the ministry call that God has for me. I am determined to allow God to lead, guide, and direct me in the journey of His plan for my life. I believe that God will reveal His path for me in the journey.

DAY 30

Great God, Great God, Great God!

Psalms 143:3 (Berean Study Bible)

Great is the LORD and greatly to be praised; His greatness is unsearchable.

So, what is greatness? Do you now know the meaning of the word *greatness*? How do you define *greatness* when thinking about God's greatness? I pose these questions as part of this reading and to encourage us to begin to think about the greatness of the God we serve. The scripture says His greatness is unsearchable. For me, this suggests that His greatness is unlimited, without any boundaries or limitations. It cannot be determined or measured, and it certainly is beyond what our minds could ever comprehend.

I think God's greatness can be summarized as having true *humility to serve because of His mighty power and authority*. I come to this conclusion because when I read Mark 10:35–37, I see the complete opposite in the request of two of Jesus's disciples, who expressed their desire to be great. The Bible says the following in Mark 10:35–37 (NLT), *"Then James and John, the sons of Zebedee, came over and spoke to him. "Teacher," they said, "we want you to do us a favor." "What is your request?" he asked. They replied, "When you sit on your glorious throne, we want to sit in places of honor next to you, one on your right and the other on your left."*

I do not think these two had any idea what they were asking of our God, who is sovereign, the God who is in control of the entire universe. A God who is sovereign and yet humbles Himself to meet the needs of His people on every level. He is the God who made us righteous through the shed blood of His own Son. He is our protector. He is the God who shepherds us. He is our Creator God. He created the world by just speaking the Word.

Prayer of Faith

Father, God, thank you for being the Great God that You are. I am so grateful to be in Your family. Your name is great, and You are truly worthy of all praise, honor, and glory from all of creation. You are so deserving of all my worship. I am so grateful to have access to Jehovah the God of this whole universe. Thank you for giving so freely direct access to You. My desire is to serve You and praise You for the rest of my days here on earth. I thank You, God, for being Abba, Father to me. You are the greatest father anyone could ever have. Great God! Great God! Great God! Glory to the most High God!

Declaration of Faith

I decree and declare, He is Jehovah God, the Great God! There is no other God like Him. He is the only wise and faithful God. He is the God who loves with an everlasting love.

DAY 31

Glory, Honor, and Praise to Our God

Ephesians 3:20 (NKJV)

Now to Him who is able to do exceedingly abundantly above all that we ask or think, according to the power that works in us, to Him be glory in the Church by Christ Jesus to all generations, forever and ever. Amen.

Finally, as this prayer devotional comes to a close, I need you to remember that we serve a God who is fully capable of fulfilling every promise in His Word. We can stand on the promises of His Word because every Word in the Bible is true. For the Bible says in Numbers 23:19 (KJV), *"God is not a man, that he should lie; neither the son of man, that he should repent: hath he said, and shall he not do it? or hath he spoken, and shall he not make it good?"* All that is left for us to do is to trust God and obey what He instructs us to do.

Prayer of Faith

Father, I indeed acknowledge You as God, my God, who is capable of doing so much more than I could ever imagine, ask for, or even think of. And for that I give you all the glory, honor, and praise. Lord, I also thank you for endowing me with that same great power. Your great power, that same great power at work in me. I am so grateful to be a part of Your church, the church of the Living God and to know that

I serve a God whose power is limitless. May my faith be increased just from knowing this about You.

Declaration of Faith

Make it personal and declare, Jehovah God, my God, is the only God whose power is limitless, and I know Him as my Lord and Savior! God is faithful and fully capable of fulfilling His promises to me. I trust God! I believe God. God can do more for me than I can imagine or even think.

Free Preview
Day 1: The Power of God's Wisdom
Proverbs 3:19–22 (NKJV)

Allow God's Word from the book of Proverbs to minister to you. The Word says,

The LORD by wisdom founded the earth; By understanding He established the heavens; By His knowledge the depths were broken up, And clouds drop down the dew. My son, let them not depart from your eyes—Keep sound wisdom and discretion; So they will be life to your soul And grace to your neck.

"He Is Wisdom"

Here I believe that the Lord is speaking to our heart about how important His wisdom and understanding is to us. His wisdom is life sustaining and provides protection. How meticulous is our God, so much so that by His wisdom He created the world and us in it? Why would we not want His wisdom to guide us through the cares of this life each moment throughout our day?

ABOUT THE AUTHOR

Deborah Riley is a retired clinical social worker who worked for the Department of Defense for over thirty-two years. Her work with the Department of Defense, in her role as social worker, included working with military families in the areas of domestic violence and child abuse. She has a Bachelor of Science degree in Social Work from Morgan State University, a Master's Degree in Clinical Social Work from the University of Maryland School of Social Work and Community Planning, and a Master of Science Degree in Human Services with a Specialization in Social and Community Services from Capella University.

Deborah is a member of the National Association of Social Workers and a member of the Academy of Certified Social Workers. Deborah lives in Beaufort, South Carolina. She is a wife, mother, and grandmother.

Deborah is a member of Lighthouse Christian Center, Beaufort, South Carolina, where she serves in her capacity as a licensed minister. On occasion, Deborah facilitates the church Bible study. She also serves as women's fellowship leader in her church and head usher of the church usher ministry. She believes her calling in God's service is that of teaching. Her desire is to teach, especially women who have been abused either physically or emotionally. In this aspect of her call to teach, Deborah believes that she is to embolden and empower women in their Christian faith and God given abilities, gifts and talents for service in God's kingdom.